W9-APG-756

CHINESE CALLIGRAPHY

Over 300 CHARACTERS *of* ART *and* BEAUTY

JOSHUA HOUGH

Chinese Calligraphy
Over 300 Characters of Art and Beauty

Published by
Cadence Media
5 Broadway, Suite 201
Troy, NY 12180
United States of America

ISBN: 978-1-935355-00-7
Library of Congress information on file with Publisher

Printed in China

To the Art of Chinese Calligraphy
and the Historical Masters

Foreword

Chinese calligraphy is an art as well as a means of communication. For the Chinese, the forms of written characters are as important as their meaning. The Chinese people esteem and admire their famous calligraphers, much as Westerners admire the great artists of the Renaissance.

The earliest Chinese scripts date back to Neolithic times. These first examples of Chinese writing or calligraphy were pictographs carved on pottery, bones, stone tablets, or steles. When the brush replaced the metal stylus, the art of calligraphy was born. The flexibility of the brush allowed for sensuous swoops and curves, and within a few centuries, new, artistic scripts came into use.

Just as Western languages are composed from the letters of an alphabet, Chinese ideograms (or characters) are basically composed from eight basic brushstrokes—those used in the famous character for eternity (永). Together, these eight strokes can create literally thousands of combinations. The most complex characters can contain more than forty strokes; however, they are rarely used today.

It takes many years to master the art of Chinese calligraphy. First, one must learn to sit properly and hold the brush correctly, keeping it as vertical as possible. Chinese children often practice with a duck egg. If they grip the brush correctly, the hollow space in the palm of their hand is just large enough to allow them to grip the egg. But if they hold the brush too tightly or too loosely, the egg will break, or fall.

Each character must be perfectly balanced, as if formed to fit into its own invisible square. It must be neither too large, nor too small, and all the characters in a single piece of writing may be the same or different sizes, depending on the calligraphy styles as written. Chinese children learn to write on paper that has been marked into special squares, or grids. The characters in a work also must be balanced in relation to one another, to create a spiritual consonance within the work as a whole.

Chinese characters are constructed one stroke at a time, and there is a specific order in which the strokes should be executed. Each character is built from top to bottom, and then from left to right. A person writing a character using the wrong order of strokes is considered little better than illiterate.

Proportion is everything. The strokes themselves must be perfect, neither too wide at the top nor too narrow at the base. They must not be crowded too closely together or they will "seem plagued by a thousand ailments," nor so far apart from one another that the finished character looks "like a bird soaked in water." Similarly, the finished character must be well-proportioned, neither elongated "like a dead snake hanging from a tree," nor so squat that it "resembles a frog floating on a pond."

The Chinese refer to brush, paper, ink, and inkstone as "the four precious things" or "The Four Treasures of a Scholar's Study." Chinese ink is compressed in sticks, and ground with water on an inkstone to a consistent or desired density before writing. There are many different kinds of paper, and many different kinds of brushes. When China's most famous calligrapher, Wang Xizhi, began to write a particularly important essay, it is said that he used "paper made of the silk cocoon and a brush made of mouse whiskers."

Great calligraphers develop their own individual style. Wang Xizhi was inspired by the curve of a goose's neck, and would travel miles to acquire a particularly handsome specimen. Other famous calligraphers have found inspiration in stalks of grass, or river currents.

Chinese calligraphy, painting, and poetry are intimately connected. A Chinese brush painting will often feature an inscription or a poem. Sometimes a connoisseur will add an inscription, also called a colophon, of his own.

Just as it is possible to enjoy opera without a working knowledge of Italian, one can learn to appreciate the art of Chinese calligraphy without actually being able to read Chinese. The flow, texture, and proportion of ink upon paper create a rhythmic whole that has come to be appreciated by connoisseurs all over the world.

GAIL GRAHAM, PHD, Author of *Sea Changes*

友
friend

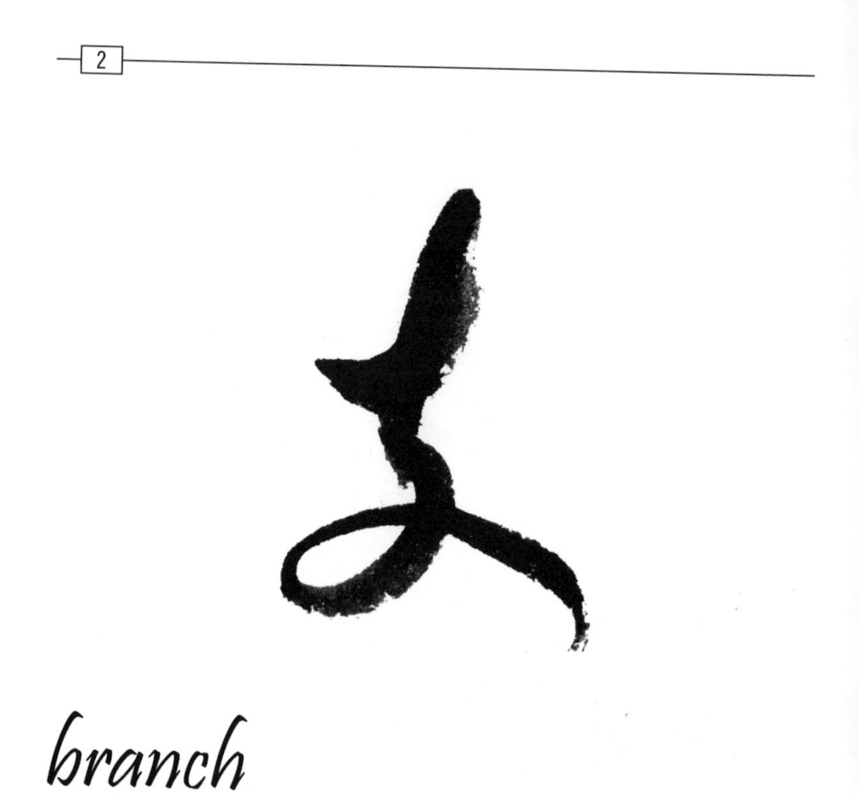

branch

好
good

hand

eternity

spiritual

rock

negativity

stone

son

soar

花
flower

愛

love

accept

祖
母
grandmother

祖父

grandfather

力
量
strength

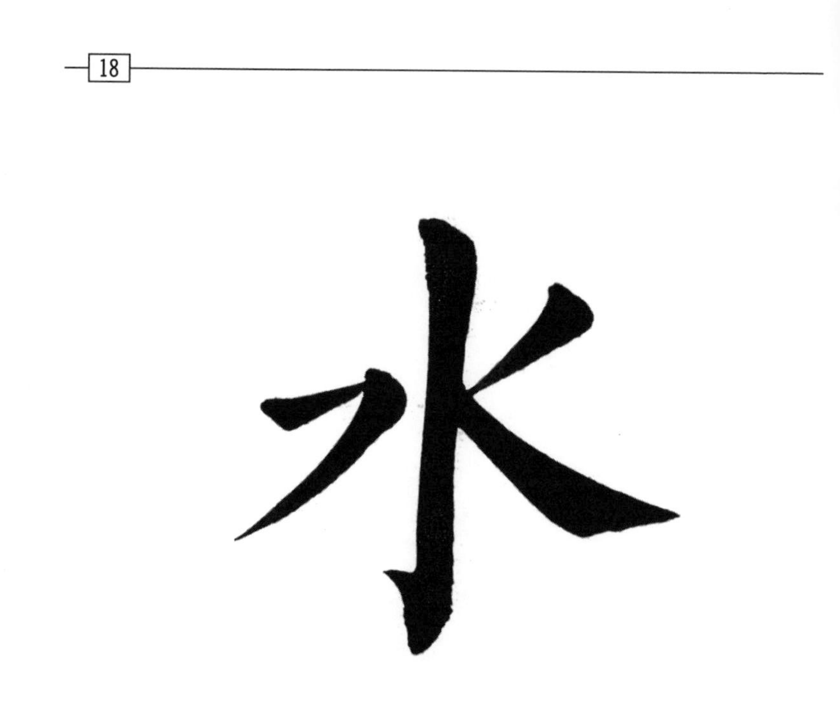

water

葉
leaf

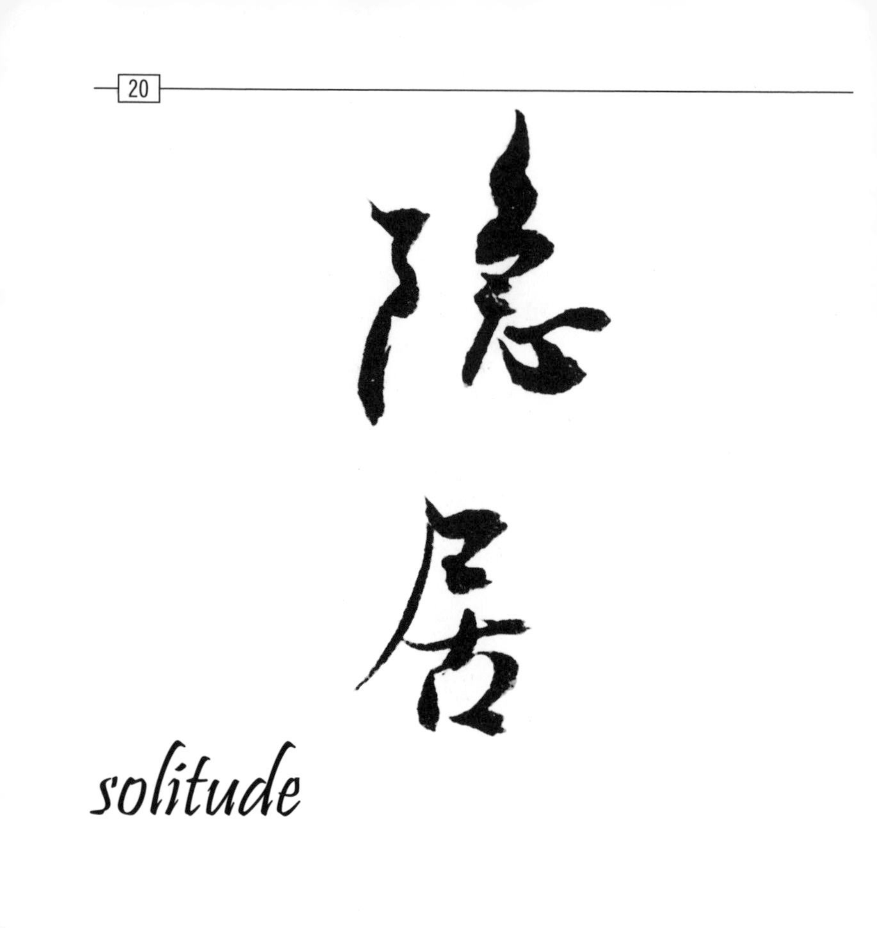
solitude

home

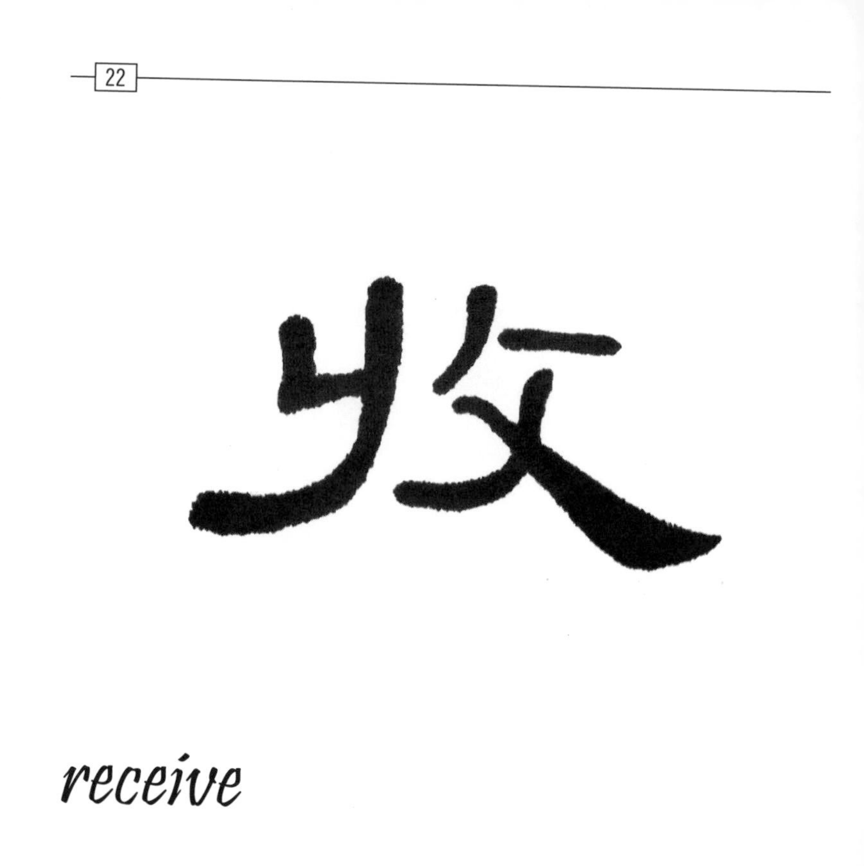
收
receive

beauty

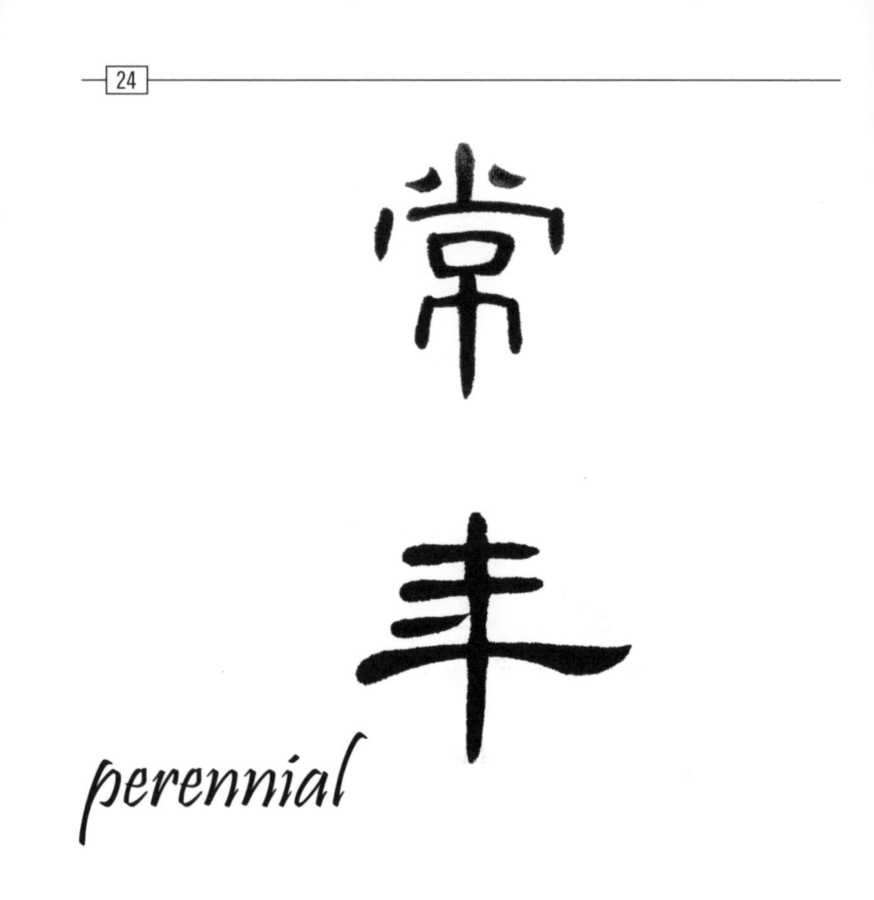
常
年
perennial

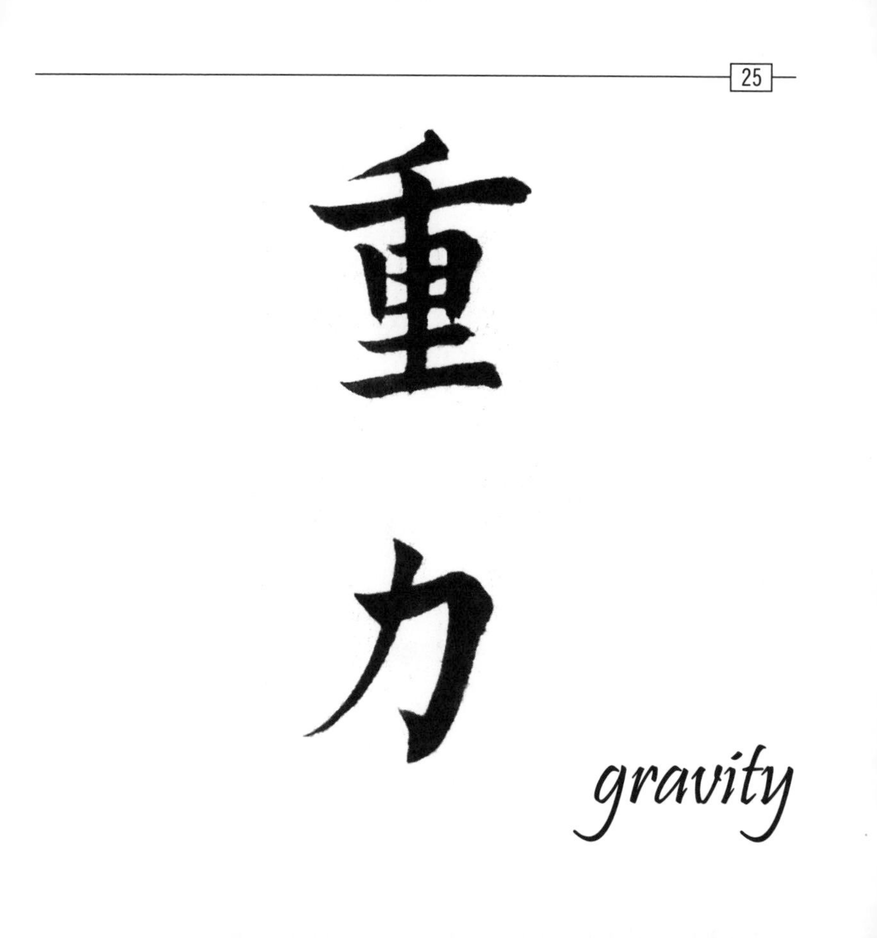
重力
gravity

touch

give

red

事
先
advance

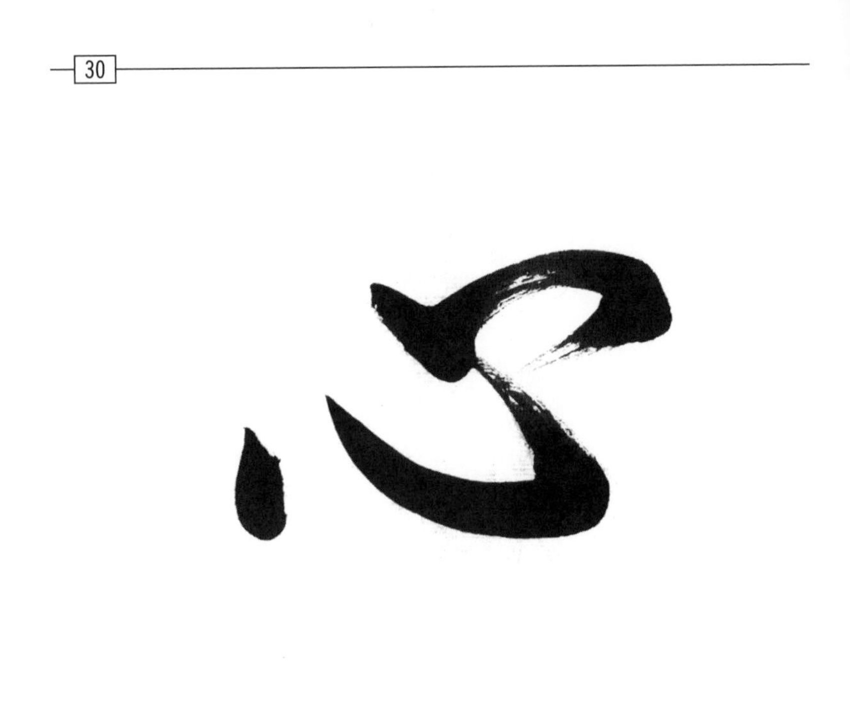

heart

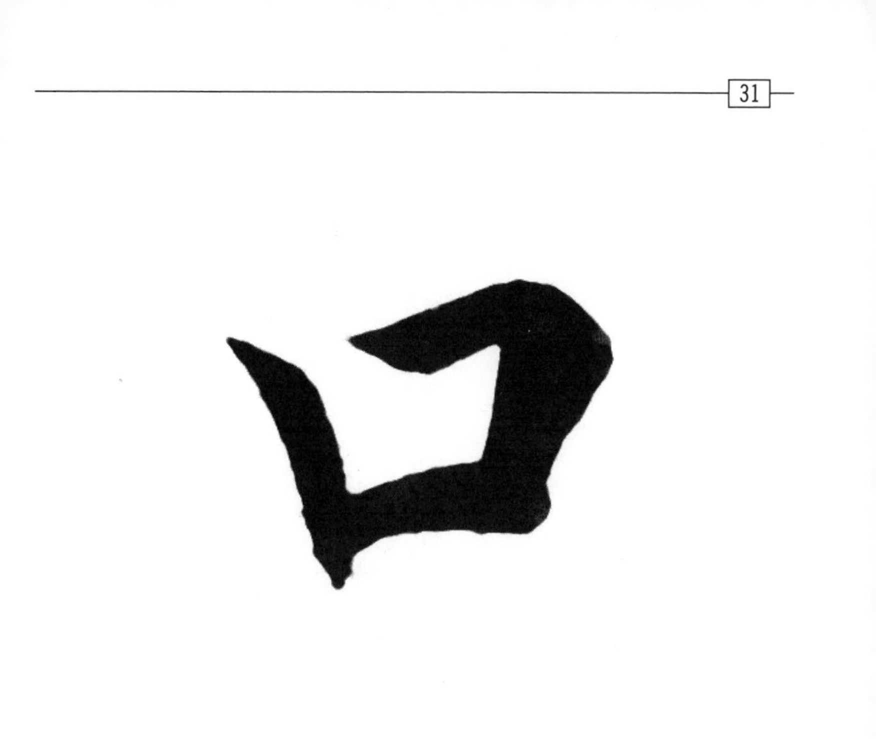

mouth

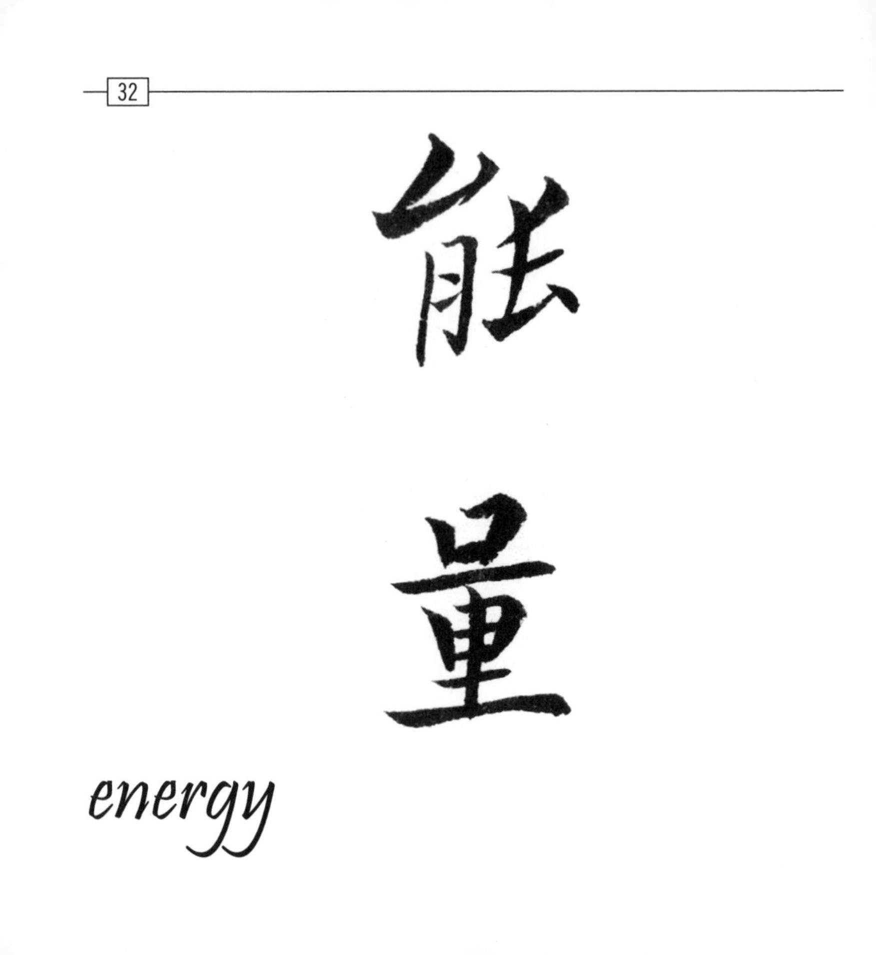

energy

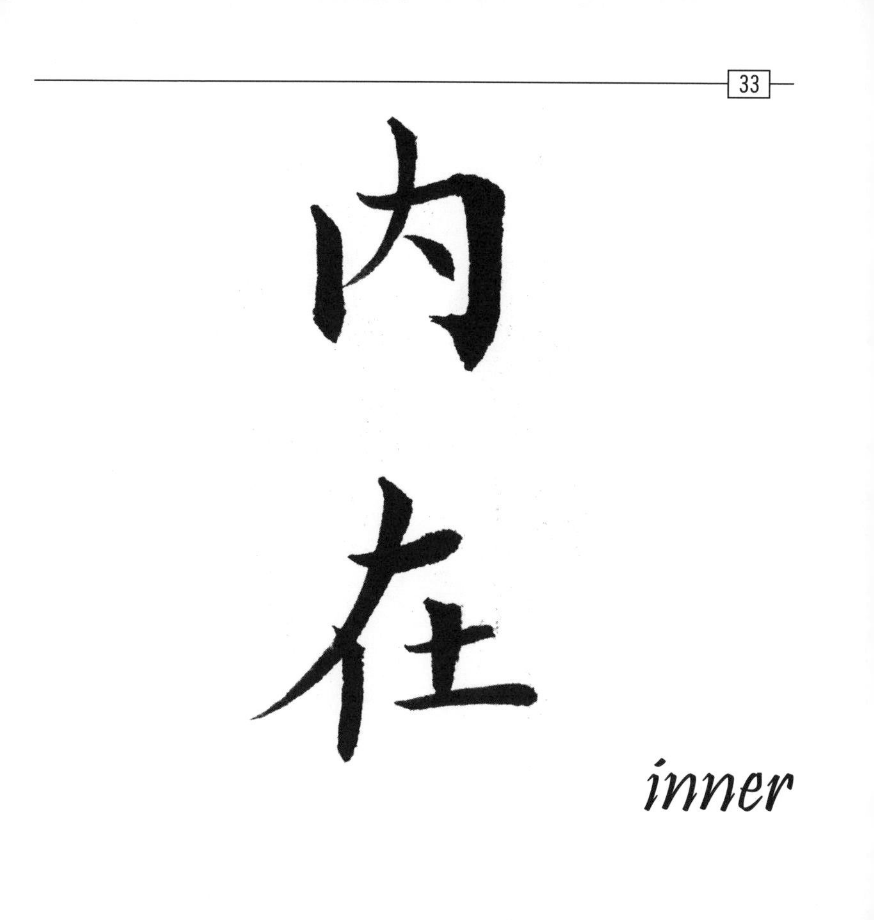
内在
inner

tree

脚
feet

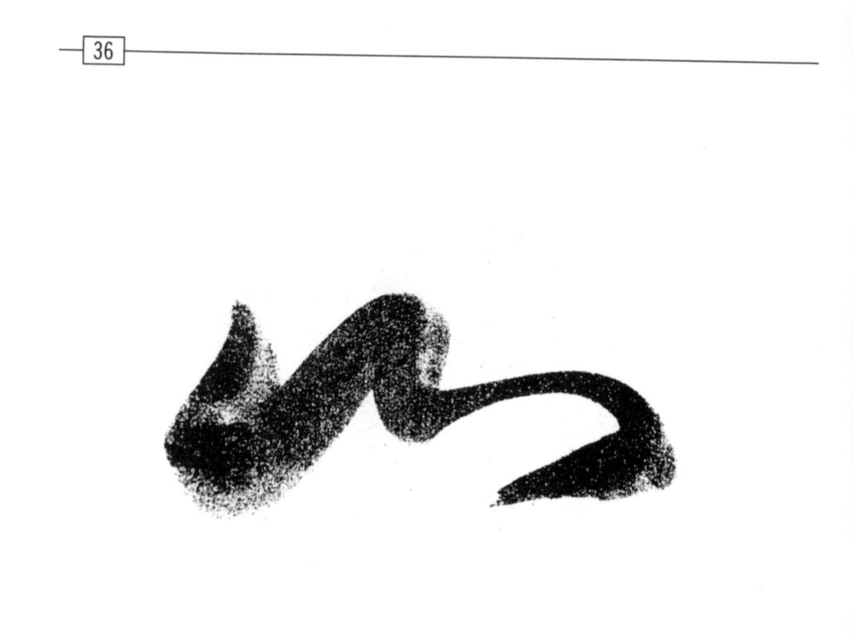

mountain

行動
action

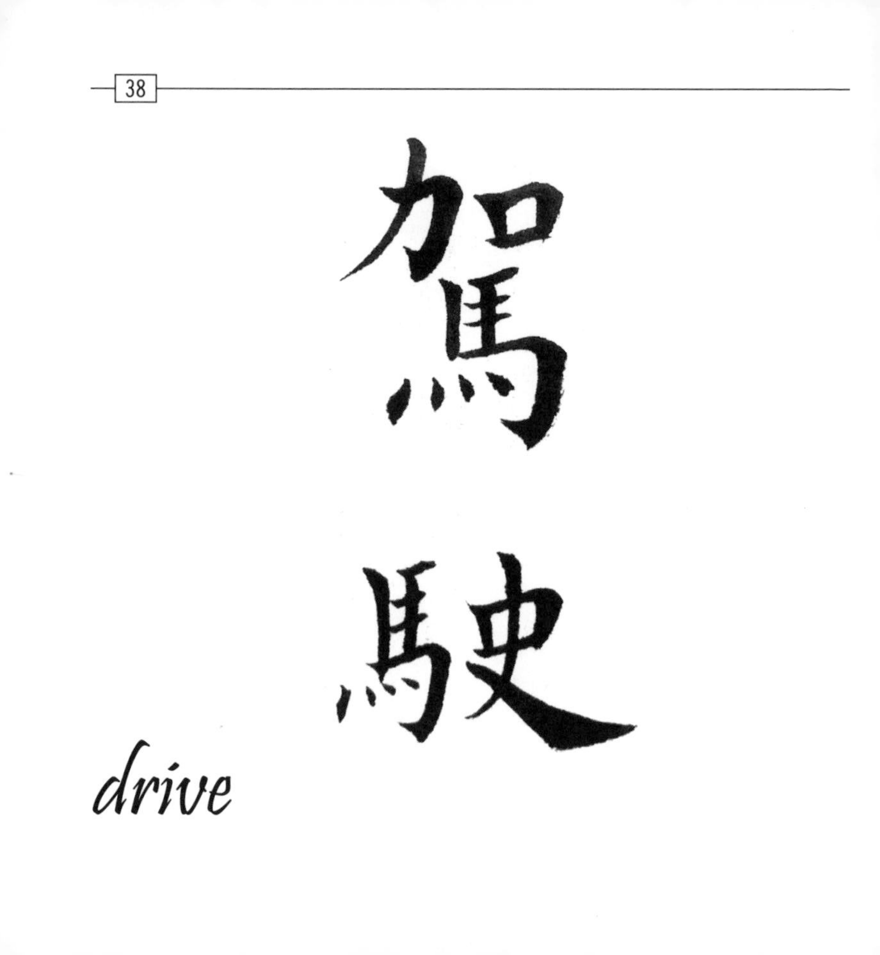

drive

master

wave

deep

最後

last

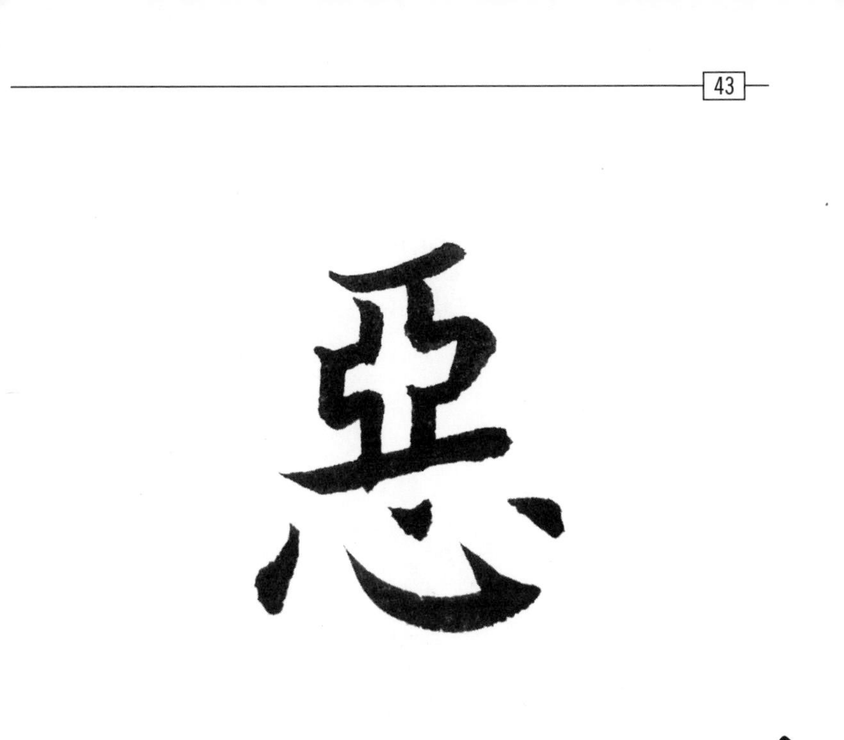

evil

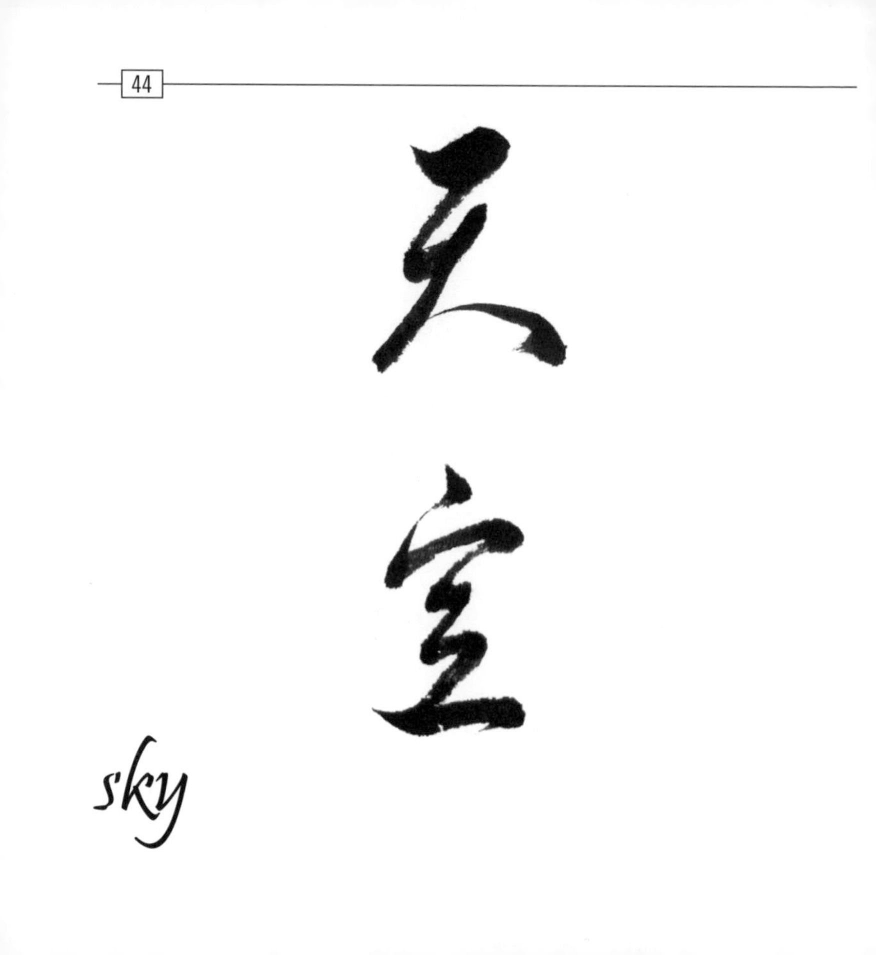
天空
sky

tea

brother

hard

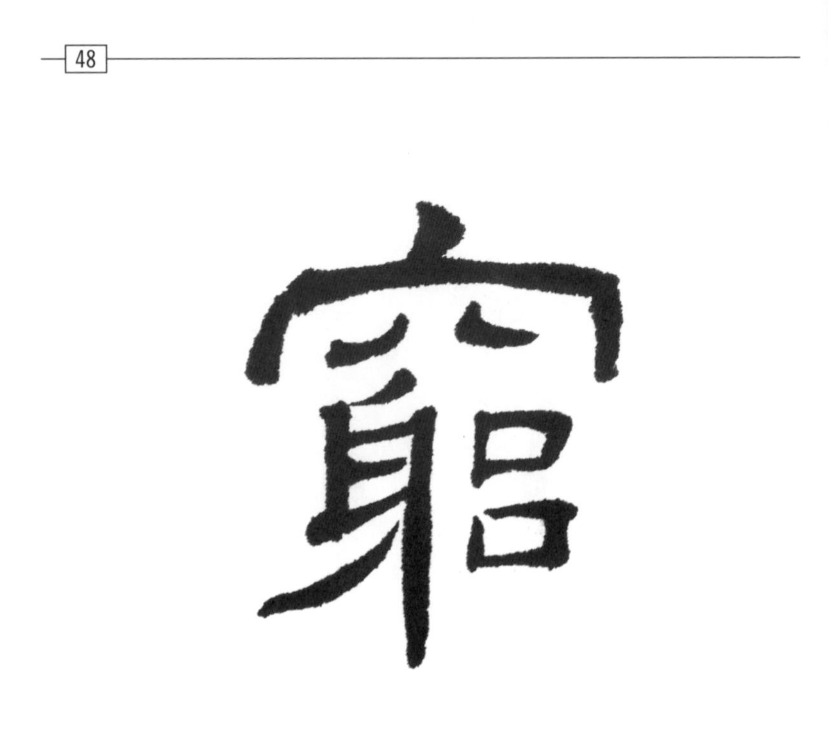

poor

靈魂
soul

night

day

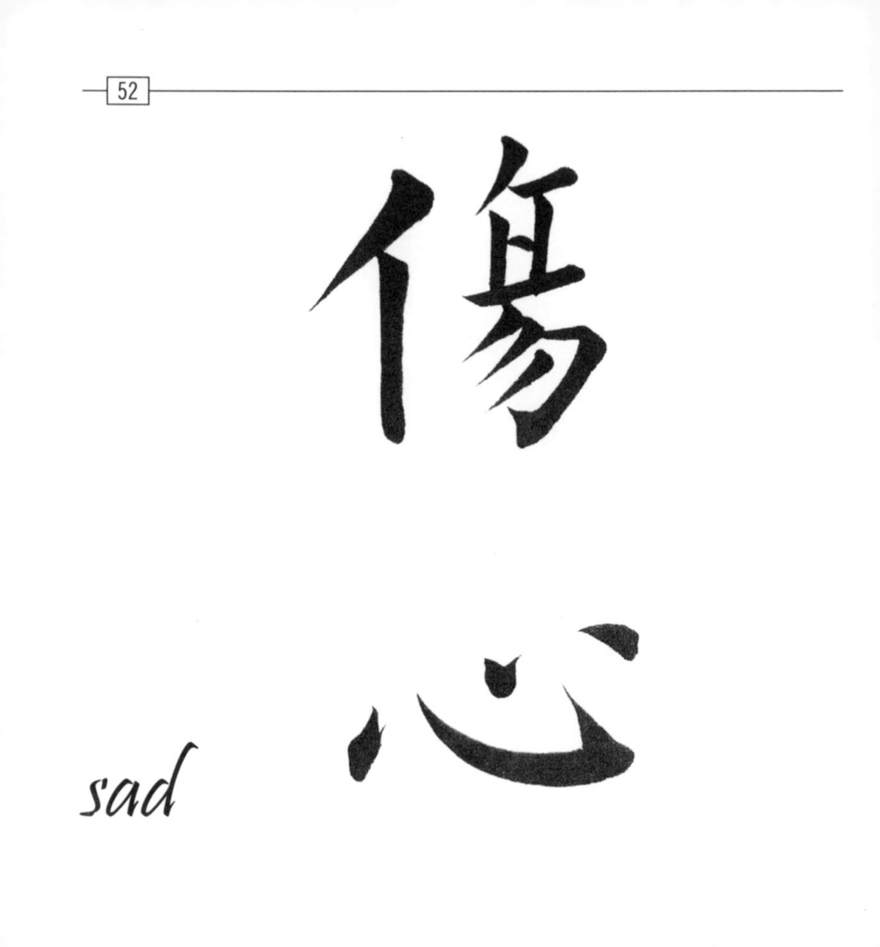
傷心
sad

受苦

suffer

dog

保護

protect

know

silver

紀

律

discipline

gain

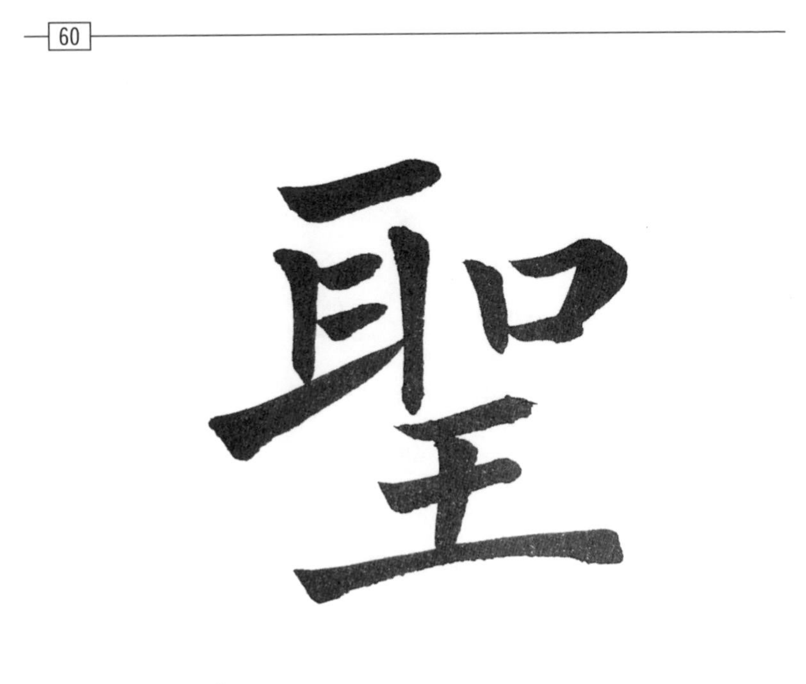

sacred

亮
bright

horse

方法
method

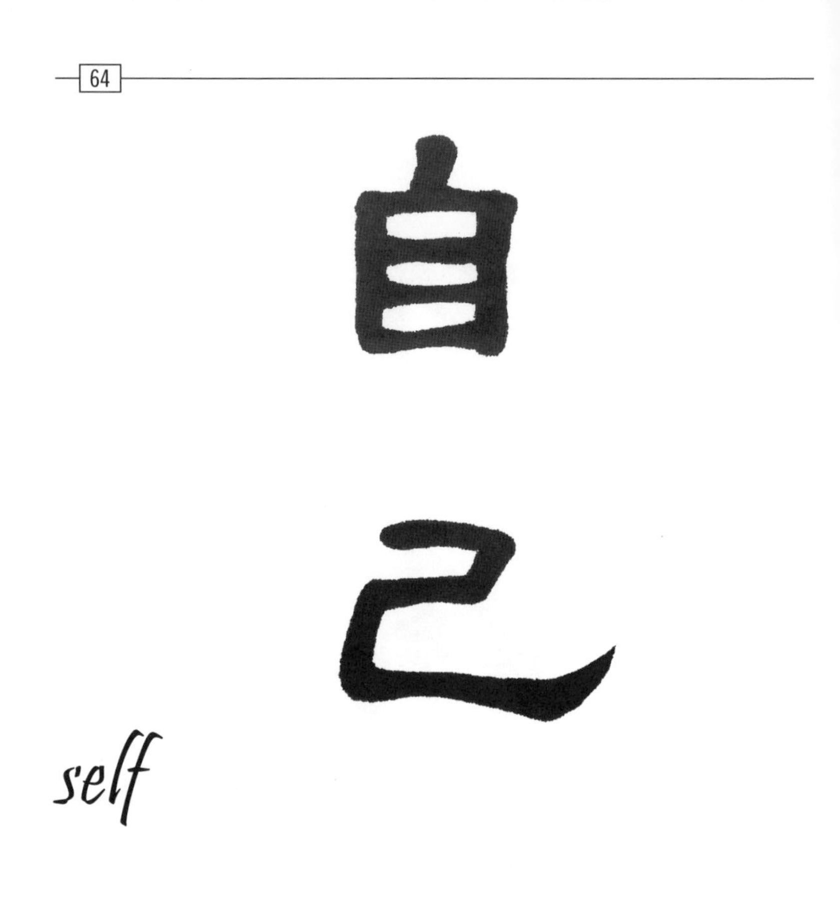
自
己
self

distraction

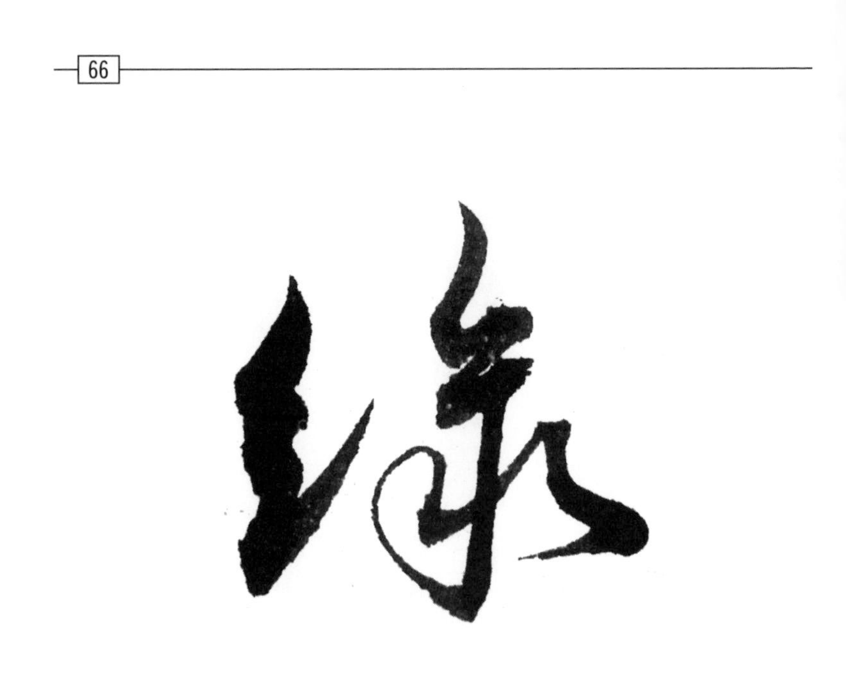

green

snow

eat

sand

drink

purple

門徒

disciple

man

健康
healthy

軟
soft

智慧

wisdom

父
親
father

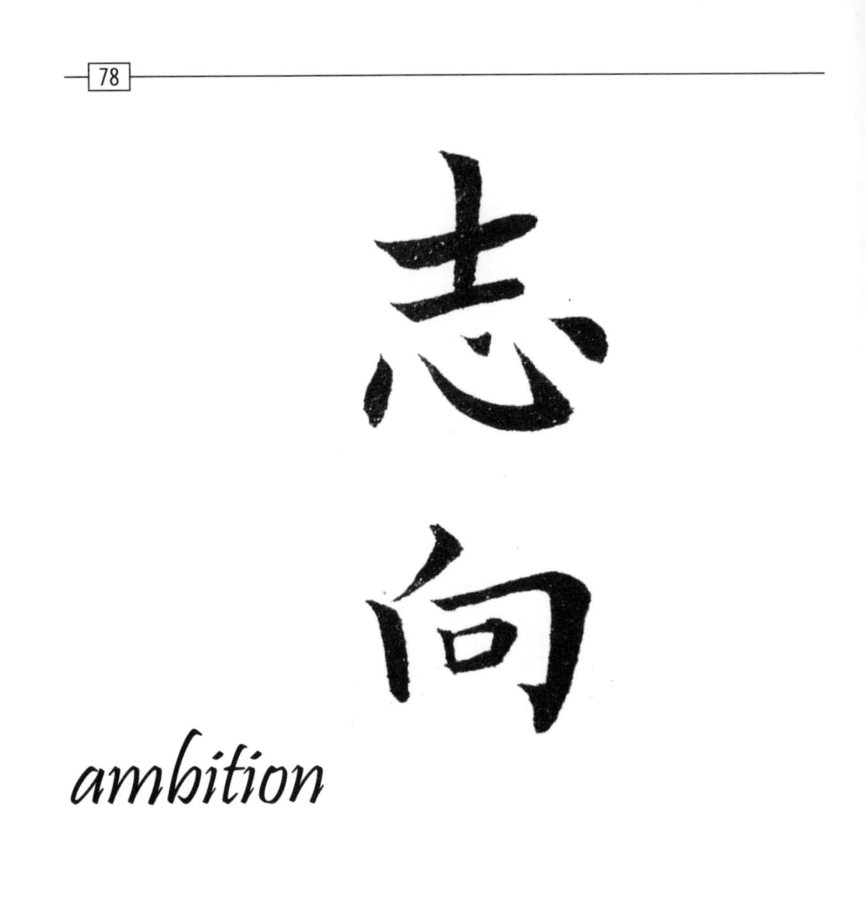

ambition

grace

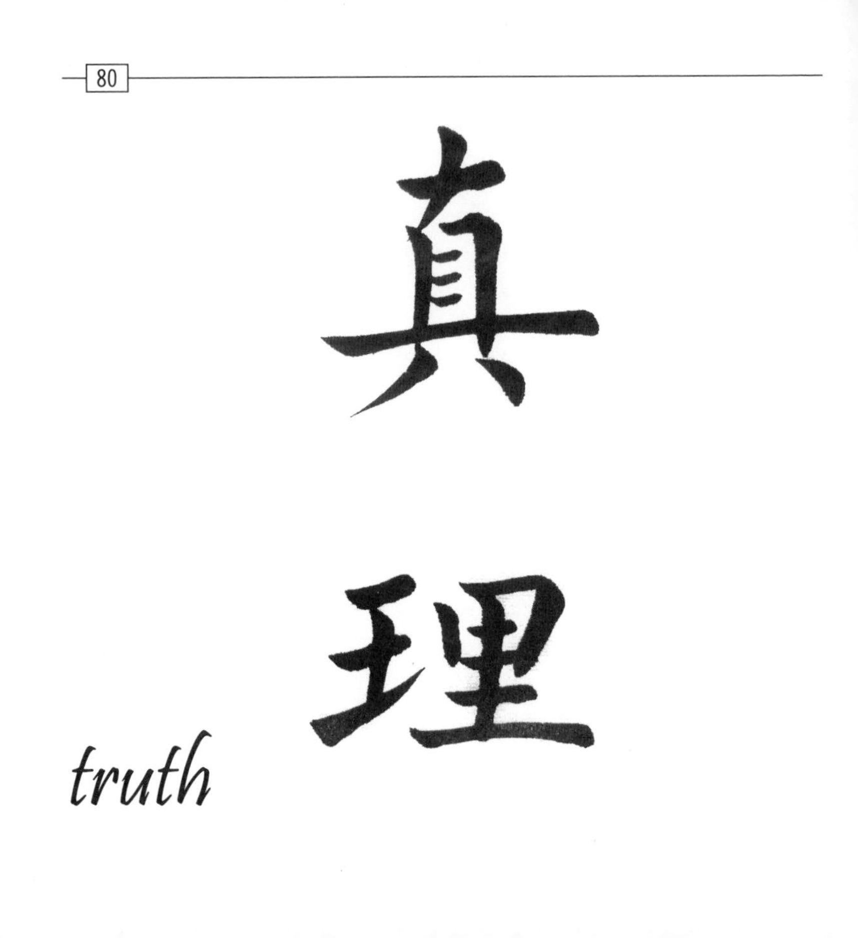
真
理
truth

passage

work

bind

完成
fulfillment

joy

sleep

導
guide

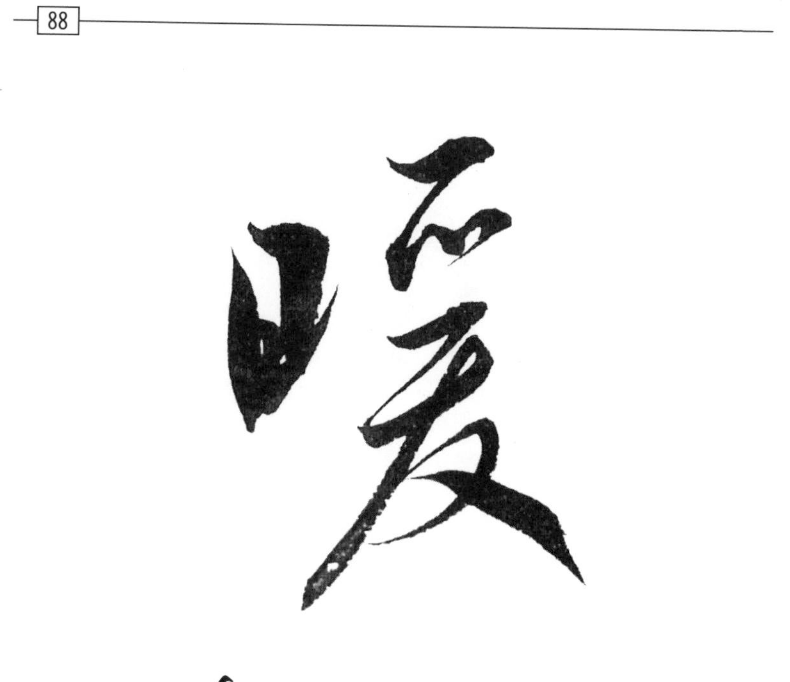

warmth

藝
術
art

desire

shell

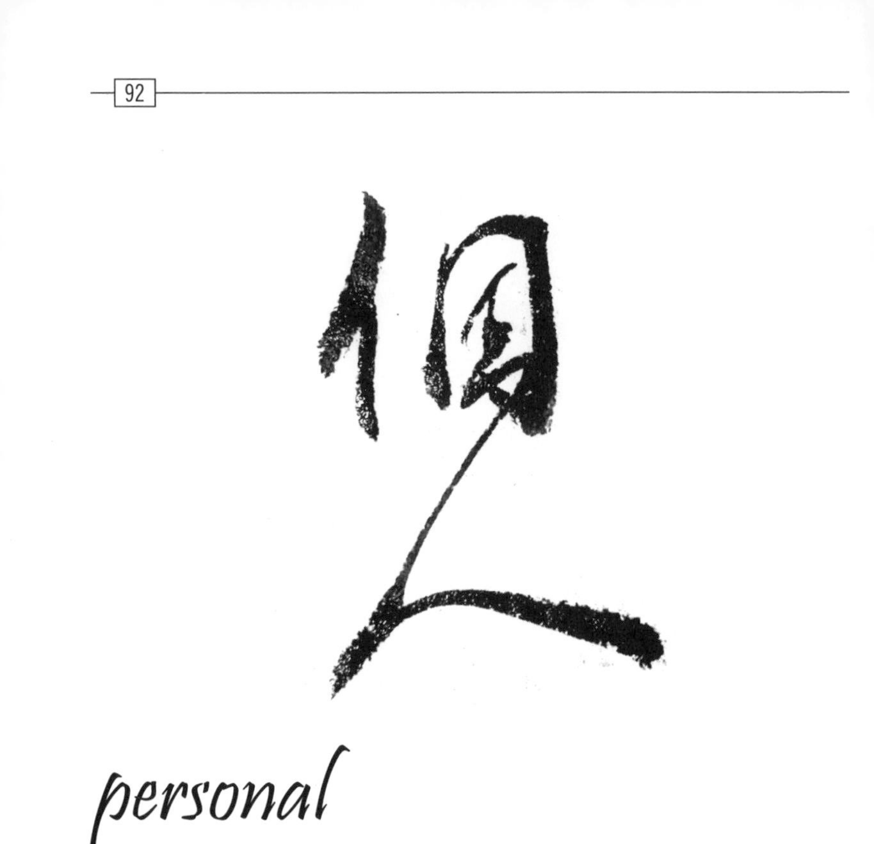

personal

determined

抱歉
sorry

island

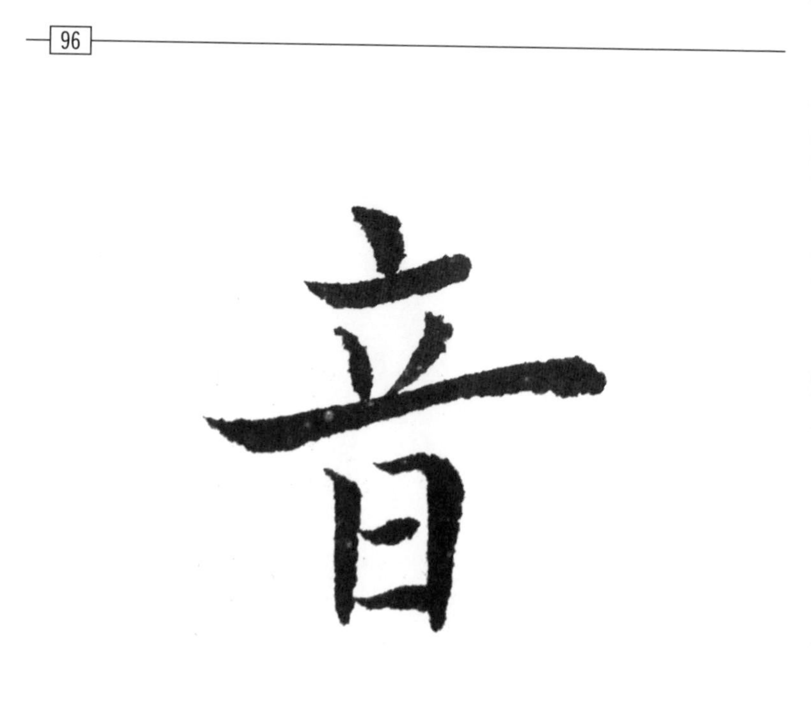

voice

放

relax

cat

無限
infinity

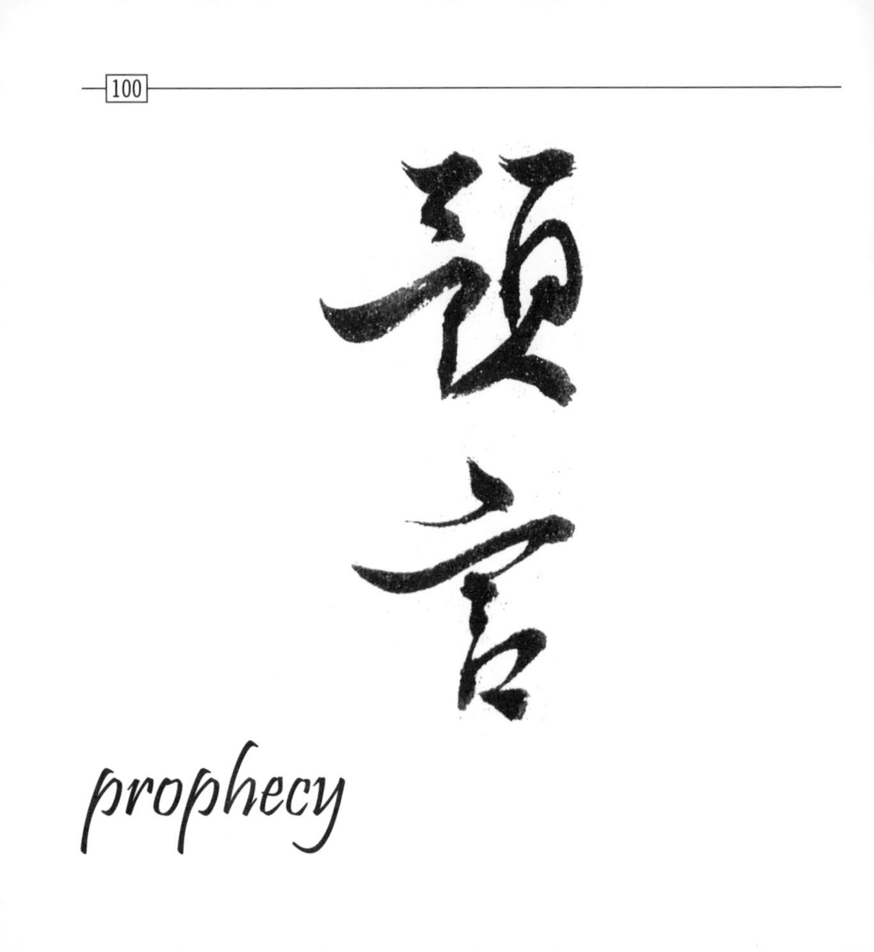
預言
prophecy

woman

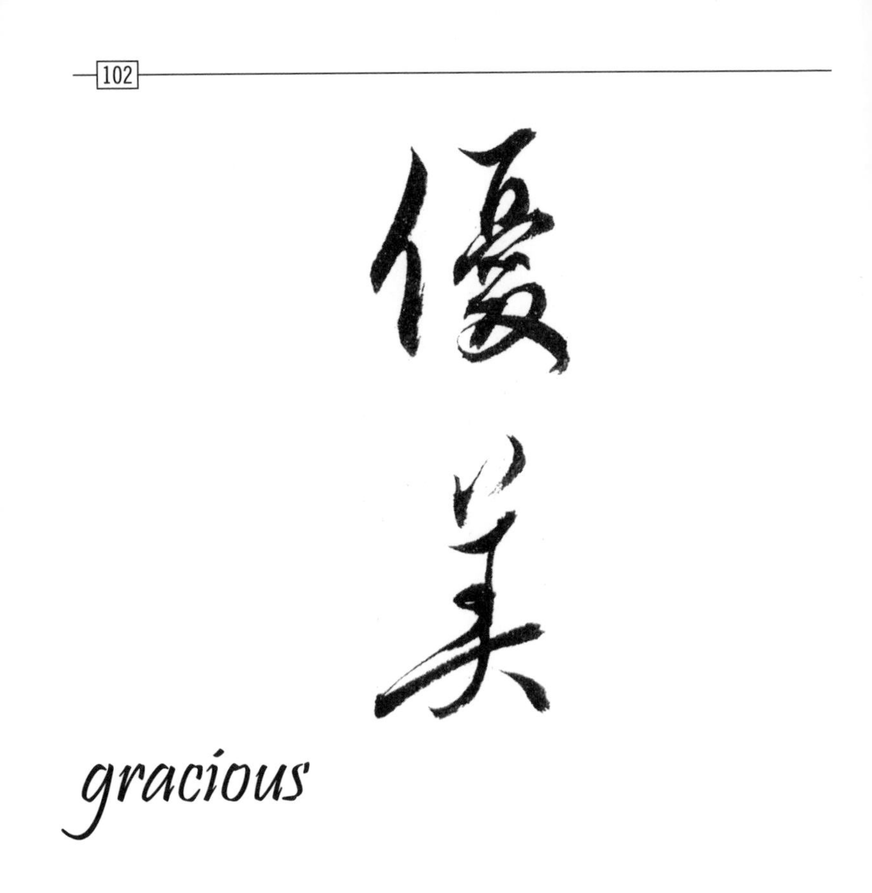
優美
gracious

sensual

awaken

serenity

vibration

創造力
creativity

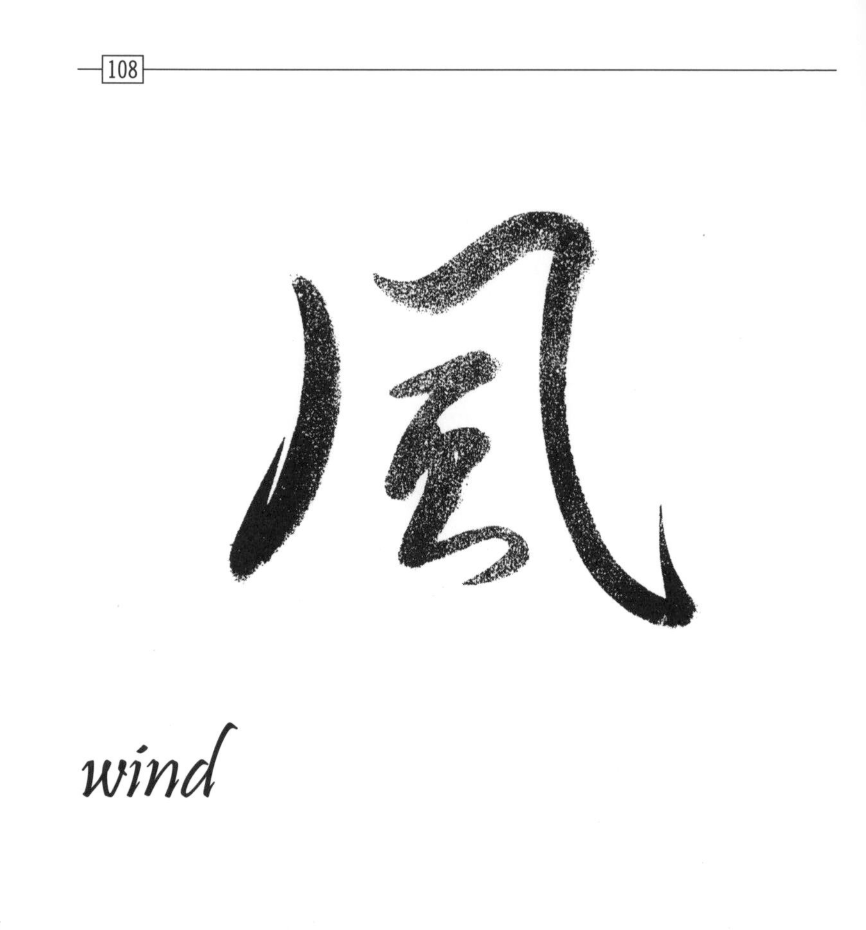

wind

physical

女
兒
daughter

形象化
visualize

諾

promise

首

first

song

旅
行

journey

富

wealth

purity

compassion

間

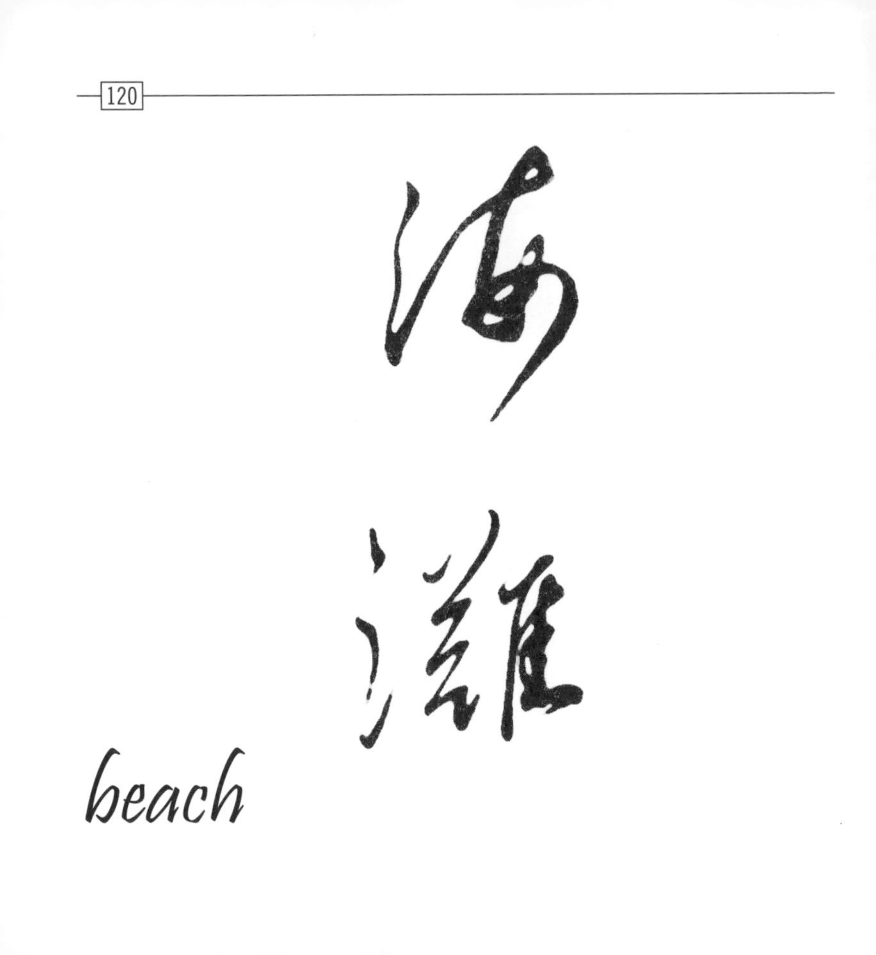

beach

surrender

help

power

content

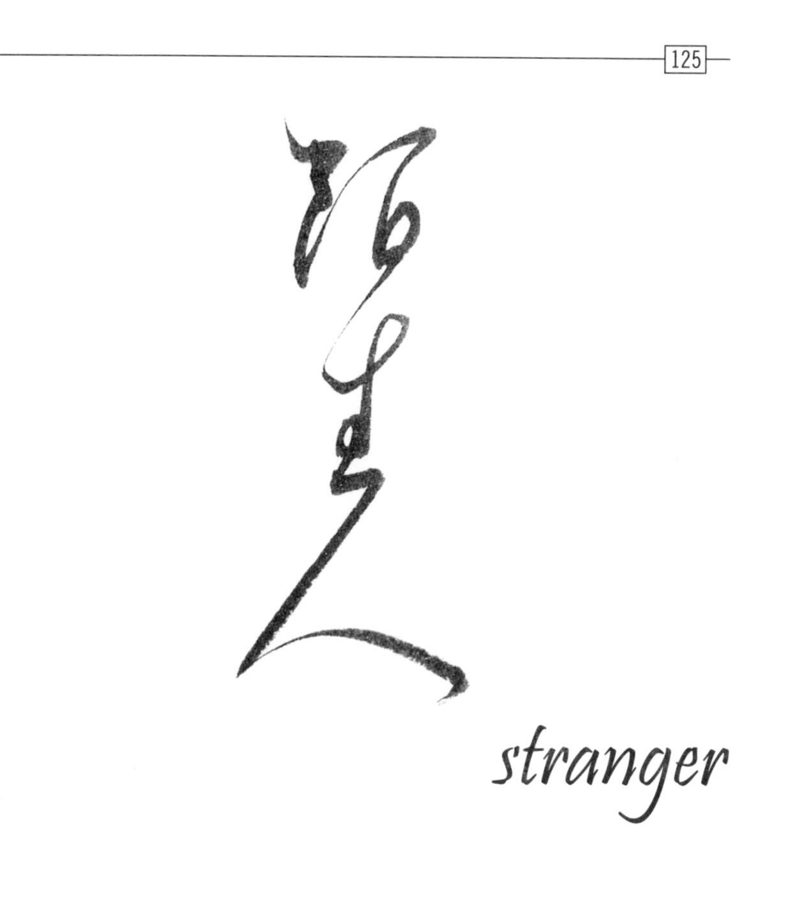

stranger

祈禱
pray

breathe

联合
unite

step

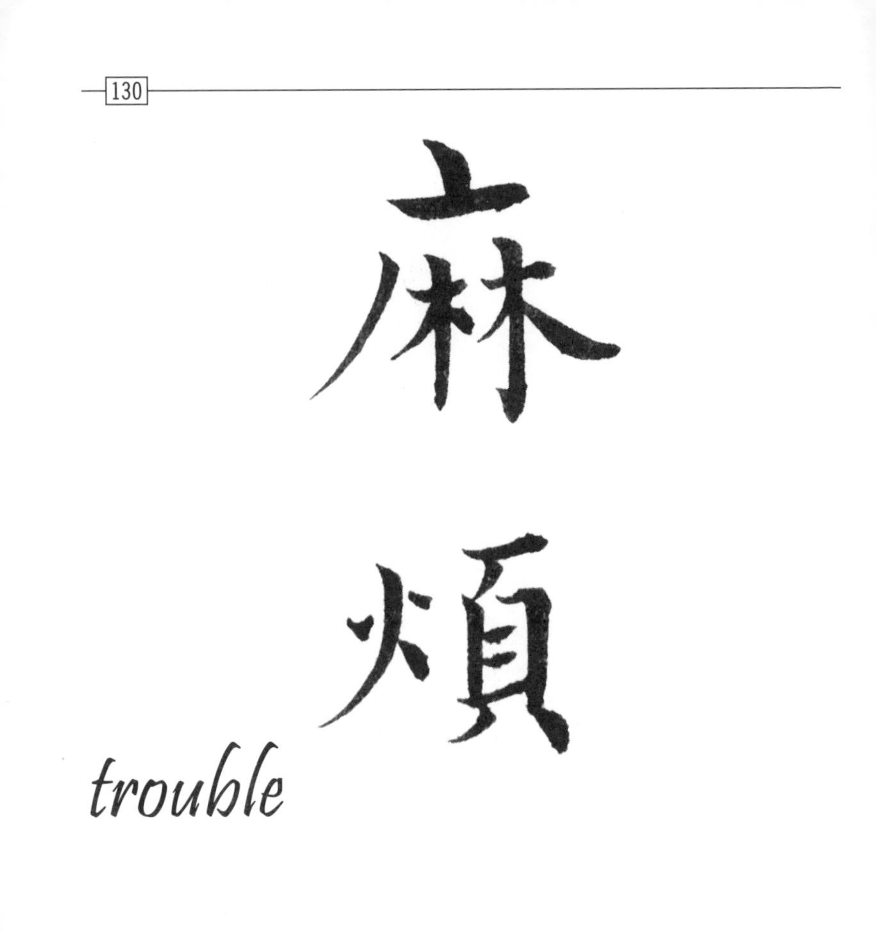
麻
煩
trouble

child

未
知
unknown

和平
peace

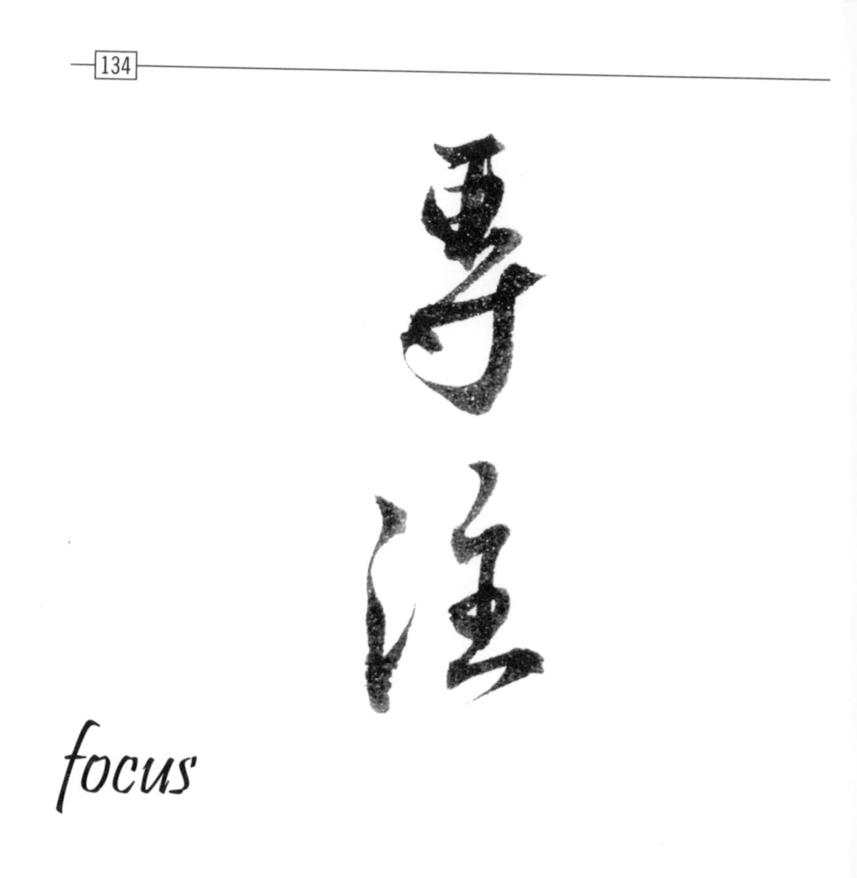

focus

姐
妹
sister

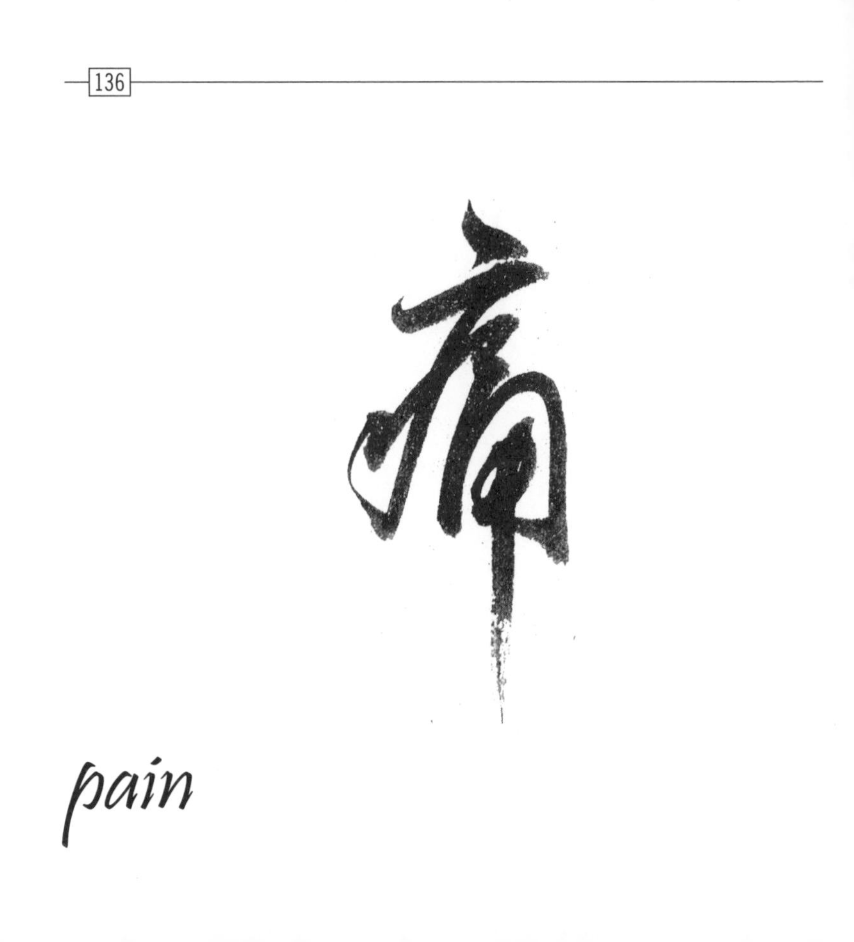
痛
pain

flow

retreat

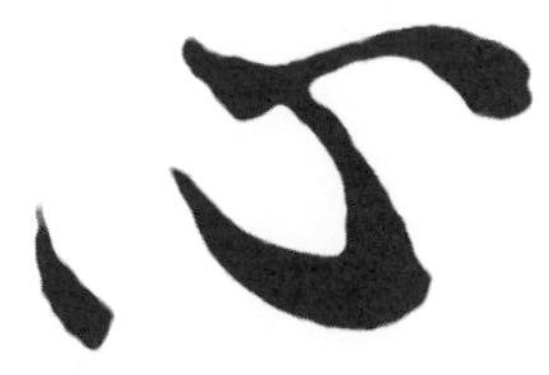

patience

calm

感

謝

gratitude

玩
play

漫

river

祝福

blessing

天
堂
heaven

安静
quiet

傳
統
traditional

pride

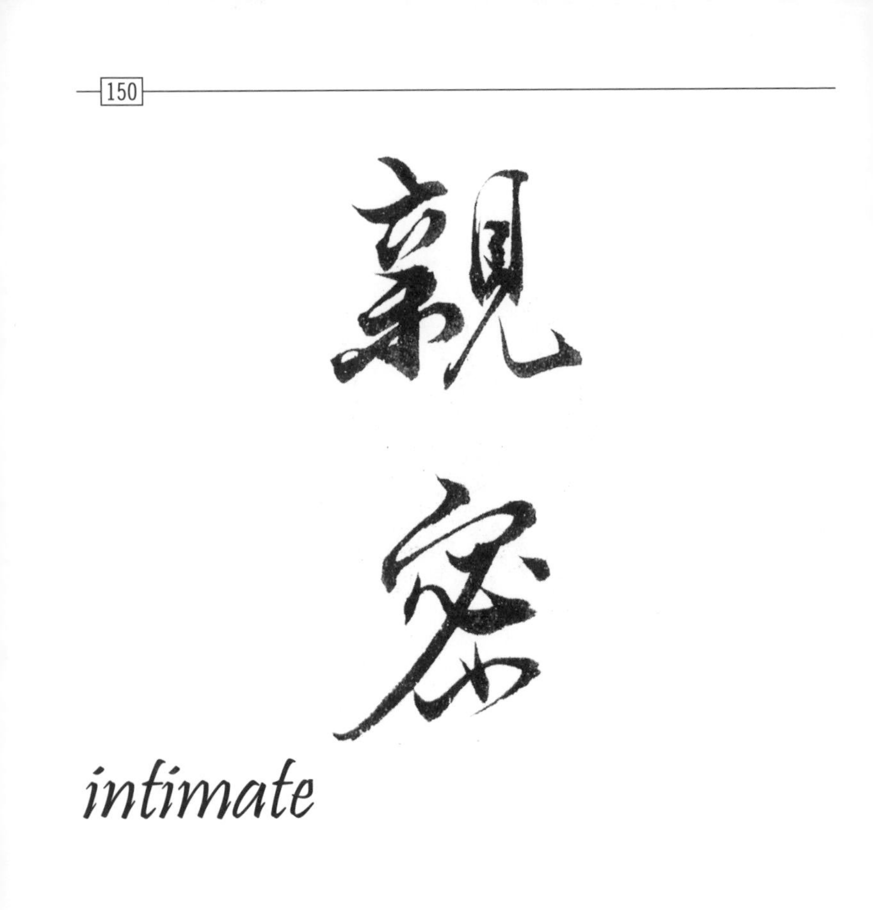

intimate

ending

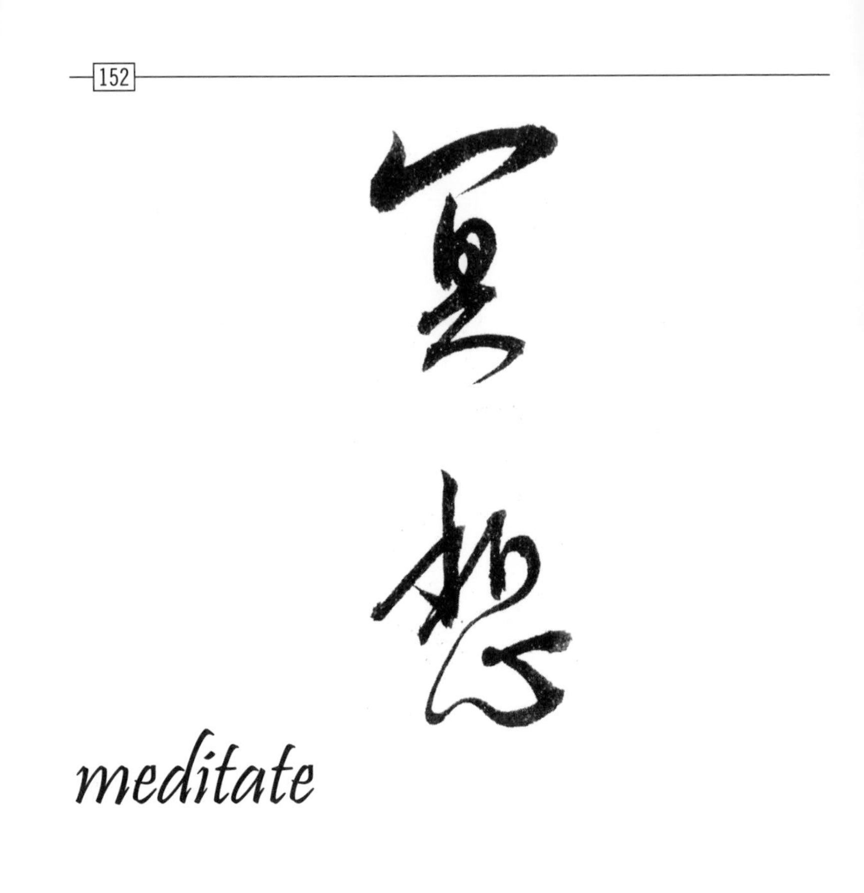
冥想
meditate

説
speak

listen

humility

dawn

伴
partner

lose

beginning

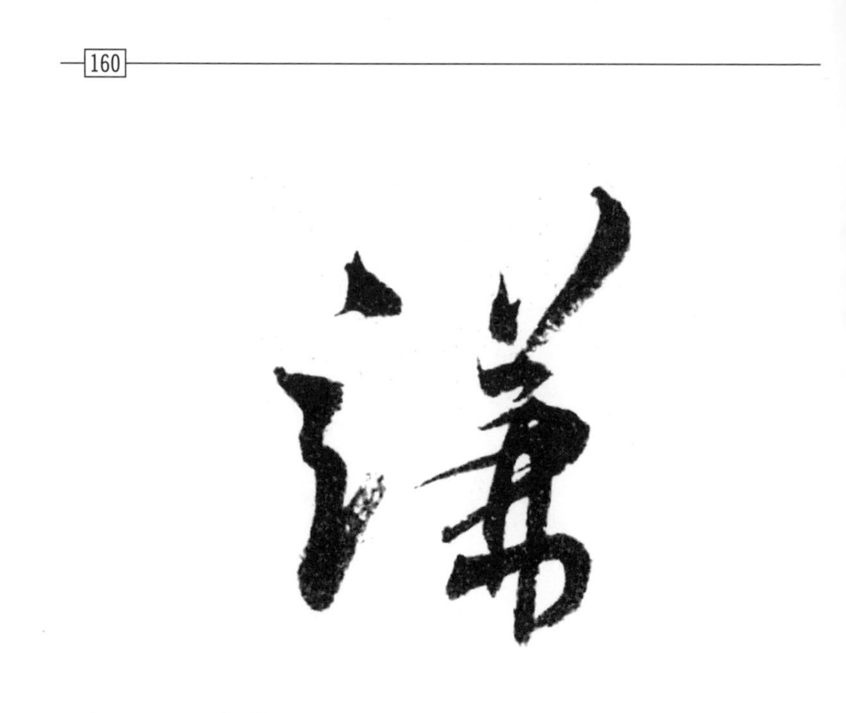

humble

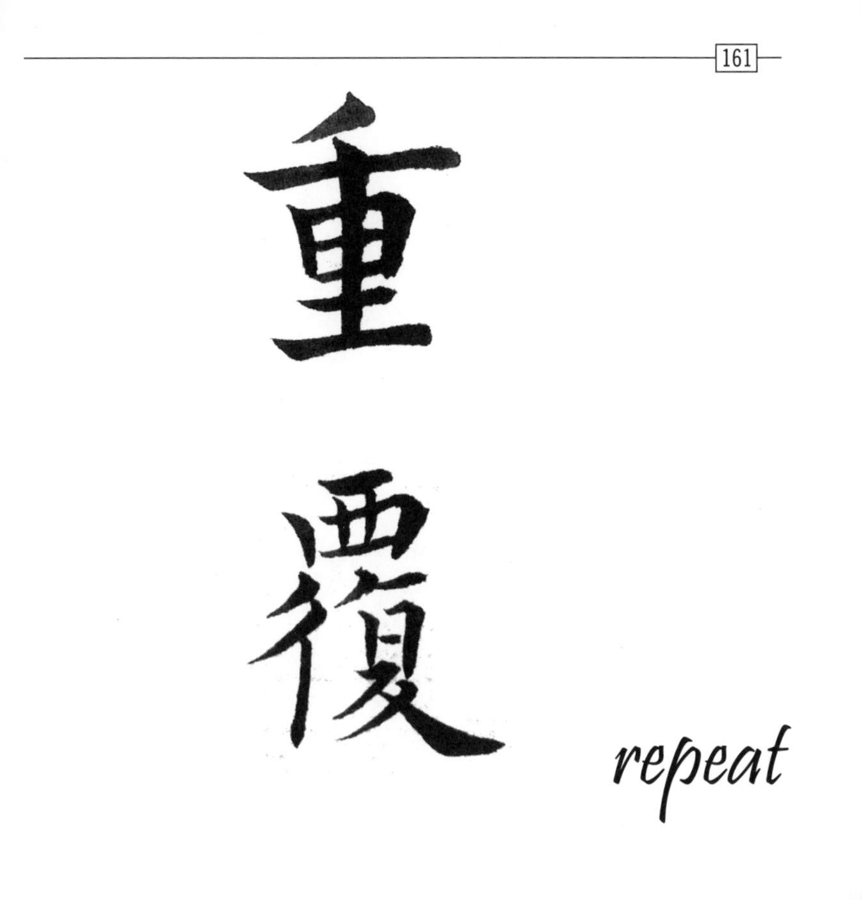
重複
repeat

intelligent

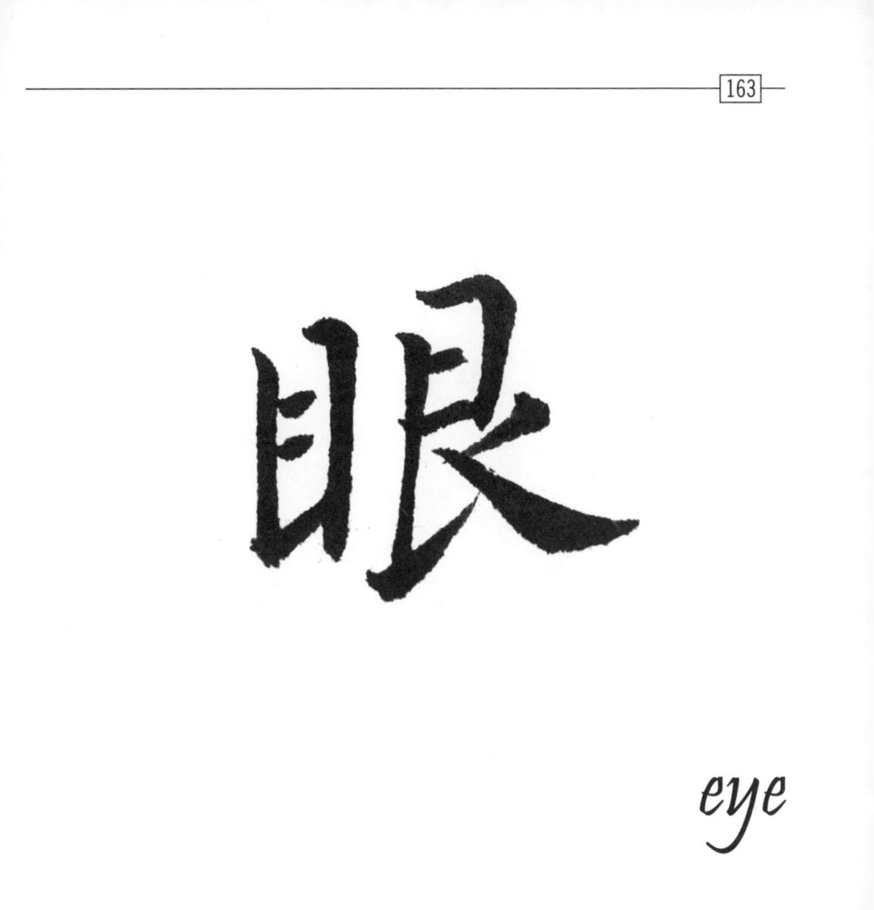
眼
eye

silent

海洋

ocean

chaos

real

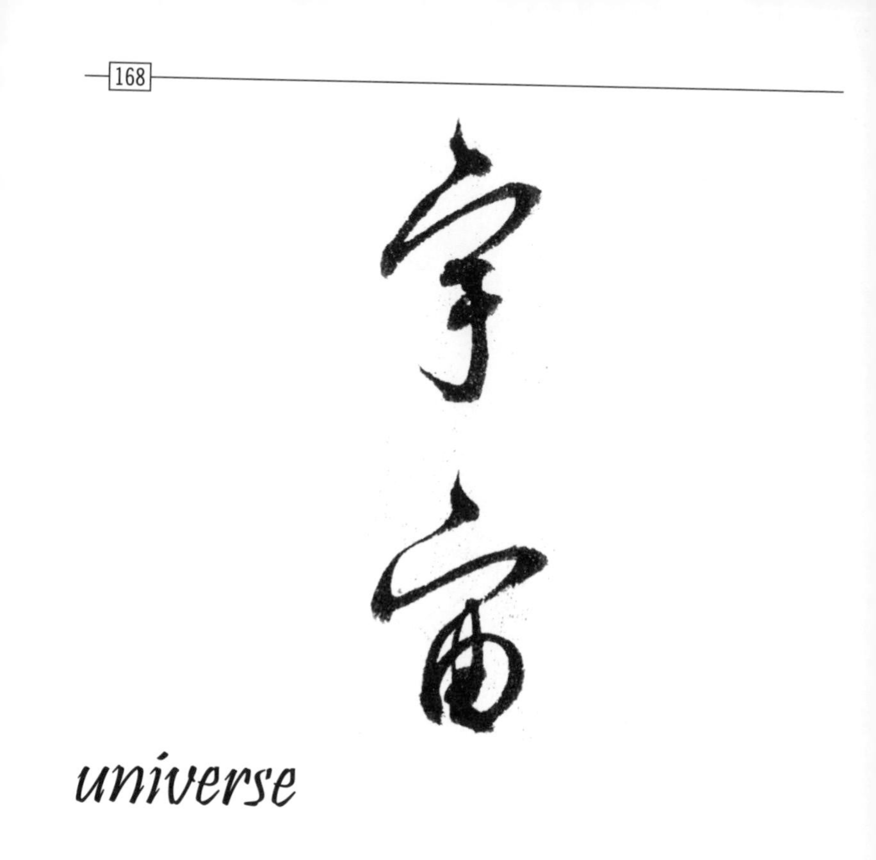
宇宙
universe

身

body

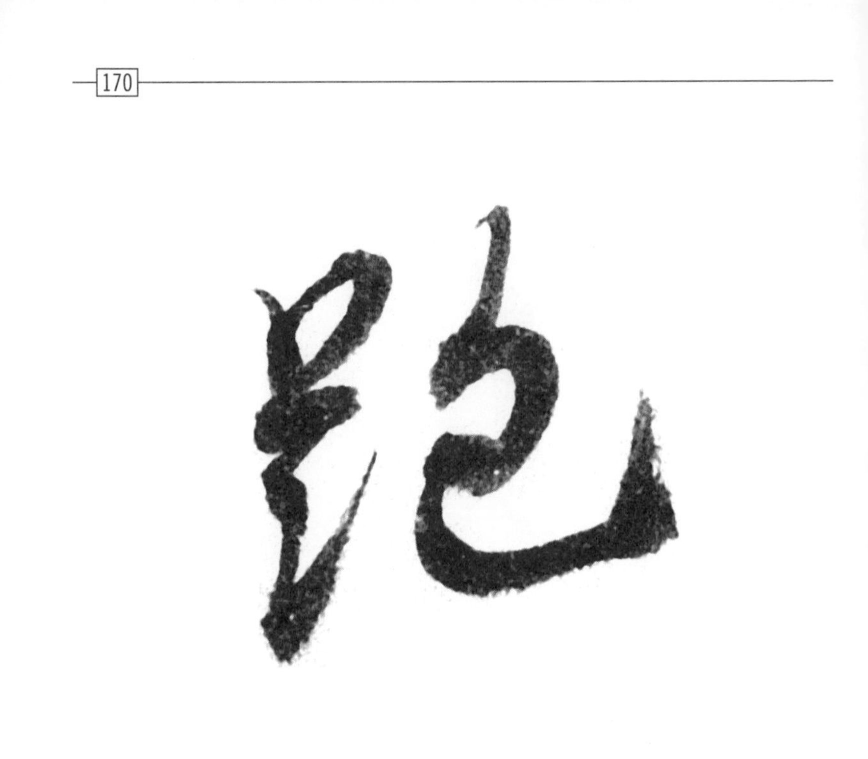

run

錢
money

jump

heal

servant

其他
other

laugh

blue

gold

領
袖
leader

旋律
rhythm

hope

essence

意識
consciousness

問
題

question

冒險
risk

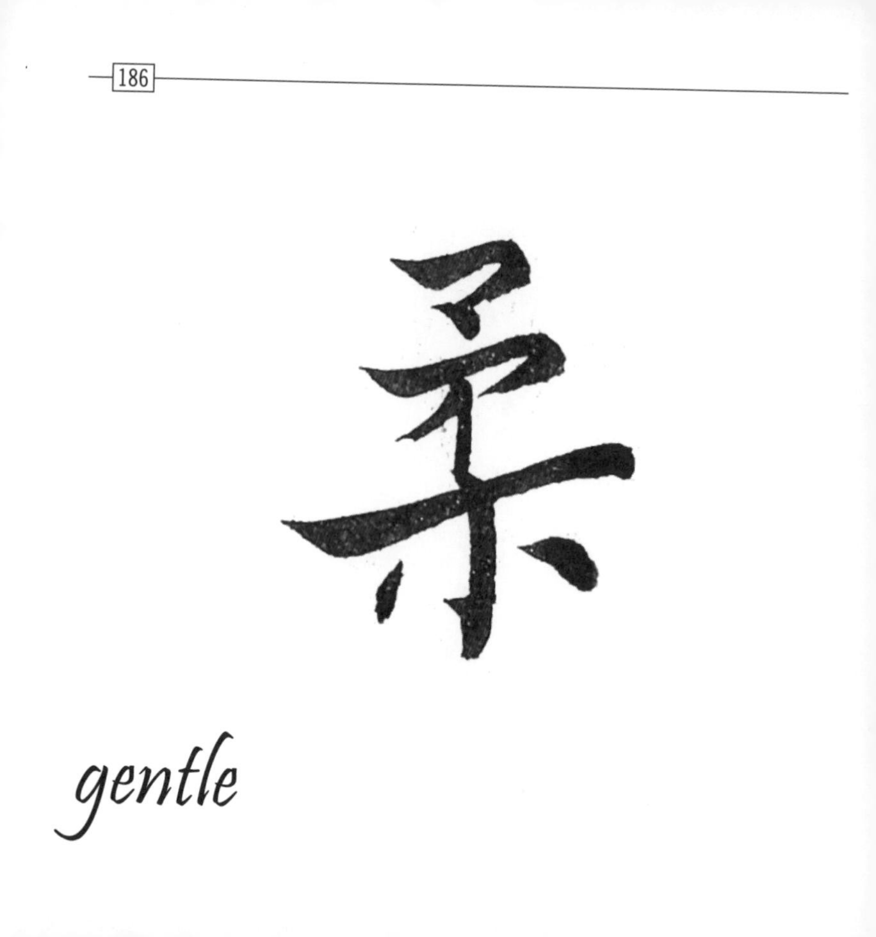

gentle

earth

省
略
skip

prosperity

mind

hide

mother

湖
lake

loss

微光
twilight

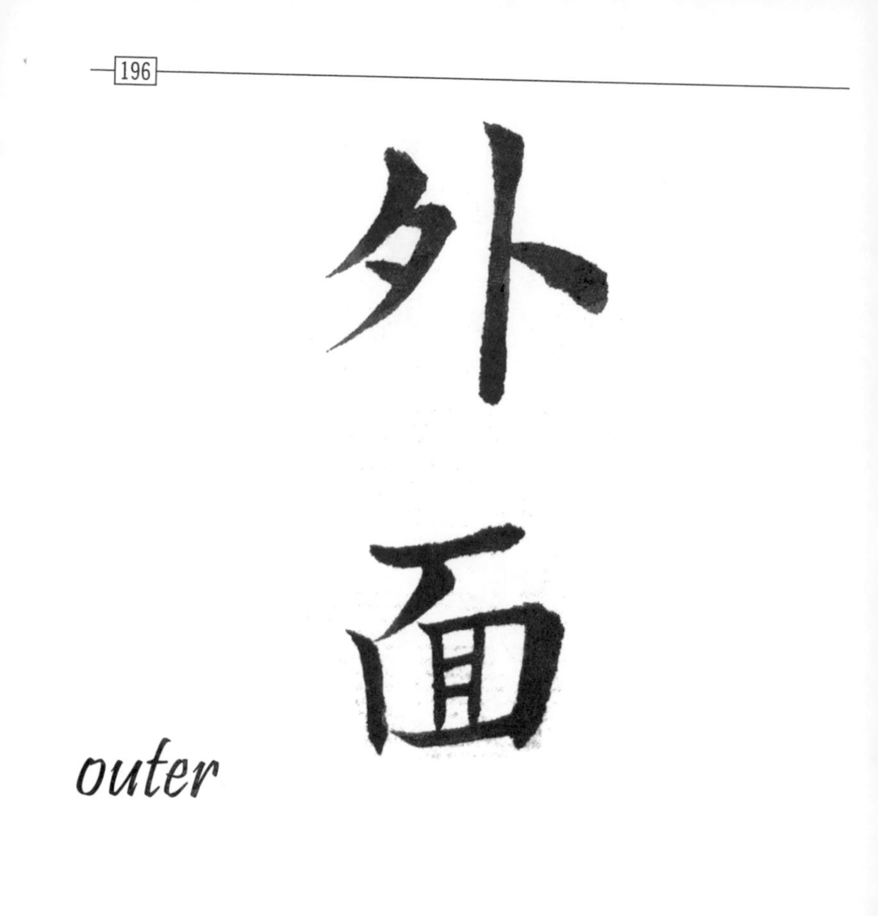
外面
outer

成
功
success

inspiration

呼
exhale

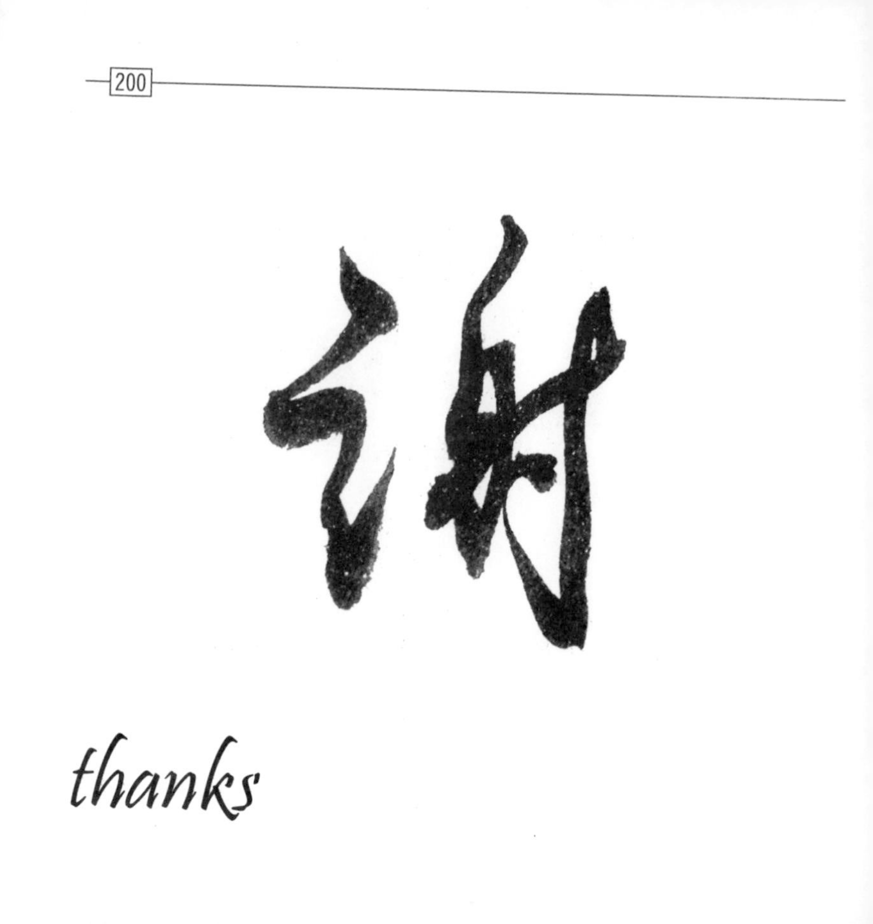
謝
thanks

Joshua Hough

Joshua Hough has been practicing Chinese calligraphy for more than twenty-five years. At a young age, he first learned General Yen Jen-Ching's Kai Style. In high school, Hough began to study Chinese calligraphy styles, history, and theories extensively and thoroughly. After Hough came to the United States, he continued his studies by learning Qigong meditation and Chinese internal martial arts to perfect his calligraphy techniques. He was fortunate to practice with several masters to learn the methodology, philosophy, and enlightenment that have enriched him in the journey of art.

In addition to his professional experience in public accounting and taxation, Hough operates the website, www.art-virtue.com, which serves as an educational resource for people who want to appreciate, learn, and practice the unique Chinese brush arts. He lives in Dallas, Texas.

About the Artist